DUMBED DOWN
DRUGGED UP
—— *and* ——
DISEMPOWERED

I0517909

AWAKENING AND MAKING THE SHIFT INTO
THE QUANTUM NEW 5D EARTH PARADIGM

A Transformational Guide to Liberate Humanity

ANDREA KAYE

© **2025 ALL RIGHTS RESERVED.**

Published by She Rises Studios Publishing **www.SheRisesStudios.com.**

No part of this book may be reproduced or transmitted in any form whatsoever, electronic, or mechanical, including photocopying, recording, or by any informational storage or retrieval system without the expressed written, dated and signed permission from the publisher and author.

LIMITS OF LIABILITY/DISCLAIMER OF WARRANTY:

The author and publisher of this book have used their best efforts in preparing this material. While every attempt has been made to verify the information provided in this book, neither the author nor the publisher assumes any responsibility for any errors, omissions, or inaccuracies.

The author and publisher make no representation or warranties with respect to the accuracy, applicability, or completeness of the contents of this book. They disclaim any warranties (expressed or implied), merchantability, or for any purpose. The author and publisher shall in no event be held liable for any loss or other damages, including but not limited to special, incidental, consequential, or other damages.

ISBN: 978-1-968061-12-8

Introduction

Holy SHIFT! I did it! I made my vision a reality. This is my story. This is my message to the world.

Humanity has been stripped of our personal power and sovereignty and conditioned to give our time, energy and attention to the very systems that control us.

We've been Dumbed Down Drugged Up and Disempowered. There is a war, a spiritual battle on the mind, the manipulation of human consciousness. The powers that be understand how our minds work, how powerful we truly are and have been hindering us from reaching our true potential.

This book is a transformational guide for truth seekers or anyone ready to embody true freedom, self love and unity consciousness to transform the world. It's evident that the world needs drastic change. Within these pages is written the truth that can, will and is liberating humanity.

Just about everything I have learned over the last decade to 15 years is written within these pages. Over the last five years specifically I have studied mindset and spirituality extensively. My certifications include Akashic Records Practitioner, NLP (neurolinguistic programming), EFT (Emotional Freedom Tapping Technique), Hypnotherapy, Life and Success Coaching, Master Certification in the Alchemy is Integrative Coaching, Intuitive Healing and I am a Certified Magnetic Mind Coach doing work with neuroplasticity and epigenetics to rewire the brain and recode DNA. I have also decided to continue my education now attending my third year at MIU, Maharishi International University, for my bachelor's in Consciousness and Human Potential.

The purpose of this book is to ignite a divine spark of remembrance within you, to awaken parts of you that have forgotten who you truly are and why you are here on this earth. Some things you read may trigger your current belief system. For some of you it will be a complete dismantling of everything you thought you knew. Understand that we must unlearn and relearn to learn the TRUTH of who we are and what we are capable of.

There is a truth in this world that is kept from us to keep humanity enslaved in fear and survival giving our time, energy and attention to the very systems that are manipulating and controlling us. My hope is that this book will awaken you to your own individual sovereignty and power so you can be part of the EVOLution rEVOLution. Truth is the power of the people is much much stronger than the people in power and love truly is the answer.

I will cover a lot in this book from the basics of quantum physics, to what mindset is and how it creates our reality, to universal law and how we can rewire our deep programmed beliefs and traumas to SHIFT our perceptions and our paradigm or the way we see and experience the world as a whole. Please keep in mind that I always encourage everyone to do their own research and form their own beliefs. Your beliefs are powerful. They create your reality. Take what resonates and leave the rest. I always say, if your beliefs are serving you well, if you are creating and living a life that you truly love or moving towards it then more power to you. If not, or if you feel there has got to be more to life than what you have been experiencing thus far, then may this book open your mind and heart to the possibility that we can create true change and transformation in the world by starting with ourselves.

Thank you for buying this book which is dedicated to my four beautiful, amazing children, their father, my partner without whom this book may not have been possible, my mother and my aunt who have always loved and supported me along the way. Also a big thank you to everyone at She Rises Studios for helping me bring my vision to life. My greatest hope and prayer is to be a guiding light in a world that was consumed by darkness; to show the world what is possible when we follow our dreams and live with passion and purpose walking boldly in our authenticity and truth. May we realize our beliefs are the only thing that separates us. "God" is Love, the glue that binds us. I love you all. Truth Love & Light. Namaste.

Table of Contents

Introduction 3

Chapter 1
How My Motherhood Journey Triggered My Awakening.................. 9

Chapter 2
The Untold TRUTH- My Story in a Nutshell 16

Chapter 3
Everything is Energy- The Basics of Quantum Physics 21

Chapter 4
Universal Law, Chakras & Consciousness 26

Chapter 5
Mindset Creates Reality 37

Chapter 6
The Five Steps to Conscious Creation 41

Chapter 7
Your Truth Your Story & Your Message Matter 48

Chapter 8
I AM Soul EVOLution - Awaken the Creator Within- How to Use All
This to Create Transformation in Ourselves & the World 52

About the Author... 59

CHAPTER 1

How My Motherhood Journey Triggered My Awakening

Hi, I'm Andrea the Magnetic Mompreneur! I'm a home birthing, unschooling mompreneur and Quantum Coach of 4 from Pennsylvania! I always knew I wanted to be a mother. It has also always been in my heart to homeschool and breastfeed my babies. I have been tandem nursing - breastfeeding two at once- now going on 10 years! It's been quite the journey getting here and now actually living it is challenging and has allowed me to grow in so many ways. I'm going to share my motherhood journey with you real quick but trigger warning- if you have any trauma related to pregnancy, reproduction or childbirth it could potentially bring up some things for you. This is my own personal experience that I choose to share because it is a huge part of who I am today.

Lots of women struggle with miscarriage and infertility. I have actually had five consecutive miscarriages prior to having my four healthy babies. Two were spontaneous, one very early in pregnancy due to a car accident, one was a blighted ovum and the last was the most traumatic experience because I expelled the fetus at home.

A blighted ovum is where a pregnancy test is positive but for unknown reasons the embryonic sack turns out to be empty. The baby never started to develop but the body somehow didn't realize for whatever reason.

My fifth and final miscarriage was the only one that I had ever been able to see the baby on an ultrasound. When I went in again at 10 weeks they could not find the heartbeat. They suggested I have everything taken out but I waited hoping for a miracle. At 14 weeks alone at home in the middle of the night, my mom on the phone, I expelled the tiny fetus. Turns out the baby had an extra chromosome and would have had down syndrome.

That was in 2012. It wasn't until 2014 that I had my first healthy full term pregnancy and had my baby boy, Amadeus Alejandro in June 2015. I had an epidural with him and a c section because they said I wasn't dilating. His name means, he who loves God is the defender of mankind. Side note, I got the name Amadeus while listening to Mozart because classical music is supposed to be good for babies' brain development in the womb!

Despite the common pressure to have continued c sections, I decided that I wanted to experience a VBAC -vaginal birth after cesarean. I birthed my daughter Leilani Amaris, which means heavenly child given by God, in a hospital meds free VBAC in August 2017. The baby girl I always wanted.

Never imagined I would be having more but in June 2020 I found out I was pregnant again and decided to have a home birth. We ended up being out of town and she was free birthed on a toilet at my in-laws February 2021. Talk about a story to tell! Valencia Brielle, means powerful warrior of God. It was always important to me that my kids have strong, unique names.

Last but definitely not least Zyan Ezekiel -little king with the strength of God. Born July 2022 free birthed at home, in the tub, with just myself, dad and siblings.

My two unassisted homebirthed babies didn't have a single pre or postnatal doctor's visit either. They are Happy Healthy & THRIVING.

I have also decided not to go the traditional route with birth certificates for my two home births. They are unregistered sovereign babies which means no birth certificates or socials. Instead they have Bibles and affidavits of birth that are notarized. Yes, they can get passports and still do everything the average American would in case you were wondering. If you want to know why I made this decision you can read the book "Your Strawman and Everything You Want to Know" to learn more about what a strawman is and how your identity is being used to make money for the systems when we sign these birth contracts.

So I often get the question, "weren't you scared that something might happen or go wrong?" My response is always, "no. I didn't allow fear into my consciousness. I simply decided what I wanted and I went for it." I didn't allow other people's past experiences or my own to keep me from creating a new future reality. I didn't allow fear to control my life.

I also get asked how my kids will get a job and pay taxes etc when they get older. Well again, I believe those systems are falling apart as we speak and will no longer exist in the not so distant future. Within the next couple of decades I predict we will create a whole new system and ways of being that are in balance with all life and creation.

I believe our children are the future leaders of the new infinite 5D earth. A new golden age for humanity to live in peace, harmony and oneness. A time where we are connected to our true divine spiritual nature of love and awakened to more of our full potential and infinite power that lies WITHIN us.

As an entrepreneur myself, I believe in the near future, many of us will no longer be working traditional jobs. Instead we will be following our dreams and passions and living a life of purpose serving one another. We will get to do what we love with the people that we love the most and live in complete abundance. Scarcity and lack, division and separation will be a thing of the past.

I have also made the decision to steer away from traditional medical practices. After doing my own extensive research and having my associates degree in the medical field, specifically having worked in pediatrics, I can honestly say we just aren't taught the truth when it comes to, well, just about everything, but definitely not in regards to true health. Let's just say we're being dumbed down, DRUGGED up and disempowered.

It was only through divine revelation that I made the decision to research the pharmaceutical industry and within a week of our first wellness visit I had made the decision not to vaccinate my children. This was a huge awakening for me.

Pharmaceutical drugs mask most underlying health issues by suppressing symptoms instead of getting to the root cause of disease and illness.

Vaccines specifically create a number of health issues that create patients for life. Less than 1% of vaccine injury is even reported to VAERS (vaccine adverse events reporting system). I have my associates in the medical field and did my internship at a pediatric clinic. I wasn't even taught about this system.

Less than 10% of that 1% is ever compensated and even with those small percentages they've given out over 4 billion dollars in tax payer money for vaccine injury since 1986. This is because of the Childhood Vaccine Injury Act of 1986 which gives blanket immunity to the industry which means no one in the making, distribution or administration of a vaccine can be held liable for vaccine injury or death, which as we have established, is drastically under reported.

Since 1986 the vaccine schedule has gone from only a few shots to over 90 on the schedule now. These vaccines are loaded with toxic chemicals and heavy metals which cause a wide variety of issues. The supreme court has even ruled them "unavoidably unsafe".

I choose not to vaccinate. All four of my children are completely unvaccinated. I believe soon more people will become aware of the dangers and risks and how they truly outweigh the so called benefits. We've been Dumbed Down, DRUGGED UP and Disempowered. Our current medical system is not about true health. It's sick care for the most part because for an industry that profits from people being sick there is no wealth in health.

Here are some links I invite and encourage you to check out for yourself:

This is all the info one needs to determine vaccines are neither safe nor effective:

1. Ingredients.
   https://www.cdc.gov/vaccines/pubs/pinkbook/downloads/append ices/B/excipient-table-2.pdf

2. Compensation for vaccine injury to date: 4,000,000,000 and counting...
   https://www.hrsa.gov/vaccine-compensation/data/index.html

3. VAERS site for vaccine injury.
   https://vaers.hhs.gov

4. HHS lawsuit that shows no safety studies have been conducted on vaccines for 39 years.
   http://icandecide.org/government/ICAN-HHS-Stipulated-Order-July-2018.pdf

5. 1986 vaccine law that shields vaccine manufacturers from liability.
   https://www.congress.gov/bill/99th-congress/house-bill/5546

6. Supreme Court rules vaccines, "unavoidably unsafe."
   https://www.supremecourt.gov/opinions/10pdf/09-152.pdf

7. HHS Vaccine Safety Responsibilities and Notice Pursuant to 42 U.S.C. § 300aa-31

http://icandecide.org/wp-content/uploads/whitepapers/ICAN%20Reply%20-%20December%2031%2C%202018.pdf

8. The Health Resources and Services Administration Vaccine Injury Table
https://www.hrsa.gov/sites/default/files/vaccinecompensation/vaccineinjurytable.pdf

9. Access to all vaccine inserts:
http://www.immunize.org/fda/

Also, a great resource:
https://vaccine.guide

There are also many other things about a traditional hospital birth I obviously didn't have to deal with having two at home. One big thing is the clamping of the umbilical cord. The baby needs that cord blood, rich in stem cells. I waited until the cord was white with 3 out of 4, had the placenta encapsulated twice and had a lotus birth with my fourth keeping the placenta connected until the cord dried on its own about 5 days. The placenta was in a special bag covered in herbs and flowers. Also the wax coating, vernix caseosa, on the baby isn't meant to be washed off. It's a coating to protect babies' delicate skin during the transition from the womb into the outside world. So yes, there's more to this but long story short, I now choose to take a more holistic approach to health and life. There is no wealth in health for an industry designed to keep people sick.

I believe we are breaking free from the current systems that are crumbling as we awaken -medical, education, government etc. even religion has played a part in the deception but we are creating a new paradigm of truly free individuals. I would love to empower any woman who has ever dreamed of experiencing a home birth that it is possible and you are far more powerful and capable than you may realize.

Motherhood, pregnancy and every stage in between in this thing called life has its challenges. It's definitely a huge learning experience and we're all just doing the best we can with the knowledge and experience we have. I strive to be a conscious parent and break the generational patterns by healing ancestral trauma. They say it runs in the family -I say this is where it runs out. I always encourage everyone to do their own research and form their own beliefs to make the best decisions for themselves and their families.

Magic and miracles exist in every moment of our everyday lives. Children are some of the best examples. They will change our lives forever and sometimes be our greatest teachers. Don't let the magic pass you by and be sure to take care of yourself along the way as we all learn and grow together.

CHAPTER 2

The Untold TRUTH- My Story in a Nutshell

Well now that you know a little about me and my motherhood journey, it's time to dive deeper into how I have come to realize the truth as I know it today. Back in 2010 I learned about this intriguing group called the Illuminati. No, I'm not a conspiracy theorist. I like to think of myself more as a conspiracy REAList. It's even the name of my YouTube channel, Conspiracy REAList YOUniverse with a capital YOU because not only are we in the universe but the universe is within you and me and everyone. I began to research and go down several "rabbit holes". You see there is a TRUTH in this world that is kept secret and hidden from the masses. There is a force, you can call it the Illuminati, the cabal, the deep state, the elites, darkness, the devil, Satan... this force has control of the human mind. It is a spiritual war on human consciousness. The powers that be know how powerful the human mind is and so we are conditioned from birth to conform to systems, ideas and beliefs about the world as we know it. We are taught the common narrative of war, poverty, sickness, scarcity, lack, separation, and division. We aren't taught about the true power and potential we possess to create our own reality. So we go about life just living unconsciously on autopilot or default based on the indoctrinated information from societal, cultural, family and religious beliefs as well as unconscious programs related to trauma.

I didn't realize all this back in 2010 but my awakening jump started after having my first child and deciding to research vaccines. Despite having my associates degree in the medical field and doing my internship at a pediatric clinic, I made the decision not to vaccinate. My intuition had kicked in major and divine revelation took over. Something told me not to do it. The information I've accumulated over the last 10 years has only further pieced together this puzzle that has brought me to believe we are being dumbed down, drugged up and disempowered.

Government, the education system, the medical industry and yes even religious institutions are all part of the systems keeping humanity suppressed. Everyone is just CONFORMING to the systems. "Be not conformed to the ways of the world but be transformed by the renewing of your mind".

You'll see me quote scripture throughout the book. I was raised as a Christian but I now see the Bible as a book of metaphysics. Meta meaning ABOVE the physical teaching us how to live according to the spirit so it cannot be taken literally from a material perspective through eyes of the flesh. I believe there is truth in all religions and that we are one body, one mind, one consciousness. We all create our own individual reality and we co-create a collective reality.

Two years later, after having my first and second child, in November 2017 I started shopping at an online wellness store and ditched toxic chemicals from my home. I learned that the typical products we use and foods we eat are loaded with toxins and genetically modified ingredients so I made the switch to safer, eco-friendly products. This is also when I really got into mindset work. Before this I had no idea what entrepreneurship or a limiting belief was. This really kick started my self discovery, self realization and personal development journey. But I wanted more. I want to know why am I here? What is my purpose? What is my potential?

So in January 2020 I decided to become a coach with the intention to have the tools to be able to help more people affordably with their mindset. I've studied all things mindset and spirituality since then. I got certified in the akashic records, NLP (neuro linguistic programming- the language of the mind), EFT (emotional freedom tapping technique), hypnotherapy, life and success coaching and a master transformational course in the alchemy of integrative coaching. I also got certified in intuitive healing. I watched countless videos online, read hundreds of books, attended courses and seminars and was just learning and growing, learning and growing. I started to study Dr. Joe Dispenza neuroplasticity, quantum physics, Bruce Lipton on epigenetics and Gregg Bradon to learn about brain and heart coherence. This all led me to the Magnetic Mind Method.

In May 2021 I came across this powerful work- The five steps to conscious creation: Superconscious Transformation Recode process, that I'll talk about more in a later chapter. It's based on proven neuroscience, epigenetics and quantum physics alongside spiritual concepts of alchemy, universal law and hermetic principles. I became certified the very next month, June 2021, a 12 week certification in only 3 weeks and I've been obsessed with the work ever since. The field of neuroscience and epigenetics is revolutionizing what psychology previously thought was possible. We now know we can rewire programs in our mind and recode our DNA to reach higher levels of human potential. Again, I'll go more into this in a later chapter.

Since using the Magnetic Mind Method I have successfully started my own coaching business from home and I've become an international and Amazon best selling author with an anthology called, Dream Big Do Bigger Build the Bridge Between Your Dreams and Reality and my chapter titled "Holy SHIFT I AM the Bridge" which of course I had to take the opportunity to be in that book when it fell into my lap because years before hand I had named my Facebook group Making Dreams Reality and it's what I'm all about- Turning Vision Into Reality. I've also been featured in "Becoming An Unstoppable Woman" magazine 3 times, Success Savvy one time, on over 20 podcasts and a speaker at four summits including "From Stuck to Unstoppable", "Conscious Mothers Rising", "Fear to Confidence" and "Girl On Fire 2023". I've built credibility and authority and have been able to reach many people with my message.

I believe what I am sharing is universal, absolute TRUTH. We are all powerful creators and we get to choose what we create. We aren't broken and we do not need to be fixed. We simply have to awaken to our own infinite power and potential within and become super conscious deliberate creators. The truth is we are creating all of this, we have just been unaware and creating unconsciously. We are taught to focus more on the material world and everything outside of us. This keeps us locked in the matrix systems, giving our time, energy and attention to them, thus this is what we create and experience.

It keeps us in fear and survival, creating from a place of separation and lack. We're stressed out, overworked and overwhelmed. Depressed about the past, anxious and worried about the future and not creating from the present moment. We neglect our inner world which, in truth, we create from the inside out- as within so without. Chaos within- chaos without. Peace within- peace without. It's all mindset. Our beliefs, thoughts, feelings, words, emotions and perceptions based on past experiences shape our reality. How we think, feel and act everyday creates our personality and our personality creates our personal reality.

I also forgot to mention that in the midst of all this I'm going through this massive spiritual awakening and really beginning to step into my own unique gifts. I had a dream about 6 years ago where I saw the seven chakras (7 Energy Centers of the Body - I'll talk about them more in an upcoming chapter) in the sky and a white Pegasus jumped through. This dream was interpreted to mean success, inner peace and freedom. I was later told I have a Pegasus guide and that Pegasus is the bringer of truth. I was also told that my whole life was about to change, that I was going to be successful beyond anything I've ever imagined and that it was going to happen so fast it would seem overwhelming – I have been watching it all unfold ever since.

There's an Untold Truth in this world. Ancient, esoteric, forbidden, hidden occult knowledge of who and what we actually are and the power and potential that lies within us. During the course of this book I will attempt to reveal everything I have learned through my experience as a seeker of truth. I've been piecing it all together and it's poured out here on the pages of this book. So here we GROW. Let's Make SHIFT Happen...

CHAPTER 3

Everything is Energy- The Basics of Quantum Physics

Nikola Tesla said, "When you think of the universe, think in terms of energy, frequency and vibration". Albert Einstein's famous equation $E=Mc^2$. At the center of all atoms are subatomic particles. Subatomic particles on an even deeper level are made of energy. In TRUTH we live in a vibrational energetic reality. Matter is an illusion. Imagine a fan that isn't in motion. There is space in between the blades. Once it is turned on it creates the illusion that the blades are one solid circular object. "Everything vibrates. Nothing is still." Again another Albert Einstein quote. Everything is particles vibrating on different frequencies creating the perception of physical matter and 3D reality. Matter is actually 99.9999999% EMPTY SPACE! Let that sink in.

So in TRUTH everything is energy. Pure creative CONSCIOUS, DIVINE energy or CONSCIOUSNESS. Our thoughts are energy. Our emotions are powerful energy in motion. Thoughts are an electrical signal and feelings are the magnetic signal. Together they create an electromagnetic field around us AKA our aura which either attracts or repels certain things into our lives. This is part of how we are creating our reality, which the majority of people have been unaware of this. It's been part of the spiritual deception taking place. There has been a war on human consciousness for control of our minds. We've been DUMBED DOWN, DRUGGED UP AND DISEMPOWERED.

TRUTH is we are energy and what we focus on expands. Where focus goes, energy flows. This is why Socrates said, "the secret to change isn't to focus our energy on fighting the old but on CREATING the new". We are CREATORS.

The powers that be the cabal, the Illuminati, the elites, the deep state, the devil, darkness, Satan or whatever you choose to call this force, knows the power of the human mind. When we are born into this world we are indoctrinated, conditioned and dare I say brainwashed with beliefs that fit the fear based agenda and narrative of the people currently "pulling the strings". We've all just been puppets. It's all a show. Depending on where you are born, cultural, societal, family and religious beliefs your paradigm or mindset can differ but for the most part we are taught to survive in a world of war, poverty, sickness, scarcity, lack, separation and division. We are taught that there isn't enough to go around and that we are separate from each other and so they keep us divided and fighting one another. They distract us with the material world giving our time, energy and attention to their systems instead of telling us of the power and potential that lies WITHIN us. We aren't taught that we have infinite power and potential through our free will and choice and power to create and so we believe them and we simply CONFORM.

TRUTH is we are beings of FREE WILL AND CHOICE. We create through free will and choice in every moment. We get to choose what we think, how we feel and the actions we take. All possibilities exist for our lives. Limitless possibilities and infinite potential- we simply have to choose. When we make a decision, time and space literally collapses and we end up on a timeline or trajectory for our lives. Had we made a different decision we might be on a completely different path. This is known as The Butterfly Effect.

Energy or spirit SOUL, what you actually are also doesn't die, it TRANSFORMS. "Death is an illusion though it be a persistent one." – Albert Einstein. So you've been here before, you just probably don't remember, unless you've done some sort of past life regression therapy or have had a massive awakening. Earth is a ground for spiritual growth and soul evolution. We come here to experience life, learn, grow, expand

and EVOLVE. It's human transformation. The human journey. We are born a pure creative spirit and then we go through the individuation process. We create individual personality identities based on our experiences and knowledge gained especially in the first few years of life when our self conscious ego is formed. We orient to the world based on these beliefs which are different depending on where we are born, family, cultural beliefs etc. At some point we have a spiritual awakening and we begin to question, awaken and remember who we are. We awaken dormant parts of ourselves and start to take our power back. We come here to master energy and creation. We come here to experience all that life has to offer, the good and the bad. Duality or polarity exists on earth so we can choose and experience it all. You may have been here many lifetimes, dealing with karmic debts, repeating the same lessons over and over. All the information from each lifetime is within you, embedded in your DNA, you see, DNA is encrypted information. They say we have so called "junk DNA" but it's simply not true. TRUTH is it's dormant and can be activated to reach higher levels of potential.

At this time we are seeing a massive awakening and SHIFT in human consciousness. This is the Age of Aquarius, the light bearer pouring new knowledge down to earth in the form of light codes from our sun. Light carries information. The Schumann resonance measures solar flares coming in from the sun. It has been off the charts in the last couple of years. These new light codes are activating our divine DNA blueprints awakening us to higher levels of self awareness, potential, divinity and consciousness. As this continues further on in our evolution humans will return to light bodies as we formally had in our ancient past.

We are channels for light and energy. God or source energy, universe, divine creative supreme intelligence, or whatever you choose to call it, works through us. Our bodies are the temple for spirit energy. It creates through US. The Chinese call it chi. The Hindus call it prana. It's all the same thing. ENERGY. You see this thing we have come to know as God,

IS energy. It is the electromagnetic pulse that runs through all of creation and gives it life.

God is love. We have all heard that before. Love is the highest vibrational frequency or energy in the YOUniverse. In the beginning was the word, and the word was God, and the word was made flesh. The word is sound, vibrations, frequencies that carry information we perceive with our 5 senses. Made in the image of this infinite eternal creative source energy, we too create with our words. The power of life and death is in the tongue. By our words we are condemned and by our words we are justified. Our words have power. Abacadara literally means I create with the words that I speak. When we vibrate on the frequency of love, speak love, and embody love, we are one with God, our true divine spiritual nature. The human journey of awakening is about the return to love, or God. To know and love thyself is to know and love God. Love is a powerful energy and the solution for a world driven by FEAR, doubt, worry, shame, bitterness, resentment, unforgiveness etc which are all low vibrational entities or energies that steal our joy, peace and life force energy. We want to be the energy we wish to attract. The goal is to embody the energy of Christ consciousness or Unity as we release the collective energies that are no longer serving us and embody higher frequencies of joy, love and peace. This is what the New 5D Earth Paradigm is all about. Out of darkness and into the light that we are. We can now consciously choose to work in flow with the laws of nature, universal laws aka the laws of "God" and all of creation.

Energy healing is also becoming increasingly popular. All illness stems from spiritual disobedience. Spiritual disobedience meaning holding on to low frequencies like anger, guilt, shame or unforgivness etc. Holding on to these spiritual energies causes physical DIS- EASE in the body.

As I stated before, our current medical system is not about true health. Holistic Regenerative Health is our future. One thing I've found along my journey has been therapeutic molecular hydrogen water which has over 2000 peer reviewed studies on the health benefits. Albert Einstein also said, "Frequencies are the medicine of the future". The hydrogen device I use is the ONLY one on the market that infuses the water with frequencies for light (it mimics photosynthesis) energy, and cell recovery. It also has magnets that align the frequency of the water with the electromagnetic field of the earth itself kicking your body back into homeostasis or balance. It is living, magnetic water. It even detoxes and cleans the blood and repairs DNA. You can find more info on my link provided at the end of the book. Frequency and energy healing is our future and the future is NOW. We can now begin to treat the root causes of disease and illness instead of just masking the symptoms.

Energy is real and can be felt Whether someone walks in the room who is having a bad day, or you are surrounded by people who inspire, empower and uplift you, you can FEEL IT. This isn't a question of science or philosophy anymore. We are multidimensional quantum beings of energy and light. This means we are not bound by time and space as we know it. "In this world but not of it." We can tune in to our intuition and higher Self, allowing us to reach more of our human potential. We can align our energy and vibration with the frequency of our desires to create and attract magic and miracles in our everyday lives.

Aligning energetically means no more chasing or forcing to make things happen in our lives. We are no longer matter trying to force matter. We become an energetic match and life just seems to flow from this space of non resistance. We are no longer creating from ego but from our hearts. Less effort is required on our part and our only goal is to be the energy we wish at attract. Like attracts like. Energy begets energy. Change your energetic signature and you change your reality just like tuning in to a different radio station or TV channel. It's all ENERGY so be mindful of the energy you emit Whether in thought, word, feeling or action. Energy always comes back to you. What you put out is mirrored and reflected back to you. Guard your hearts and minds. Protect your energy.

CHAPTER 4

Universal Law, Chakras & Consciousness

So we discovered in the last chapter that on a microscopic scale, Quantum Physics tells us that atoms or what we perceive as matter, are actually made out of energy. One unified field of consciousness sending frequencies of thought vibrations from the depths of the metaphoric ocean, and they appear on the surface of the waves of material existence.

It's a lot to take in. Holy SHIFT! There's so much more though. There are actually a whole set of universal laws that govern our world. They have been spoke about and perceived many different ways from different cultures, civilizations and religions throughout history. In this chapter I will discuss a few of them and how they work.

All this knowledge is being poured down as we enter the age of enlightenment, the age of Aquarius. We were previously in the age of Pices the fish symbol used to represent Jesus. This was an age of darkness and deception. Aquarius is the water bearer pouring knowledge upon the earth thus triggering this mass awakening aka The Great Awakening. In the grand scheme of existence, every action, thought, and event is intricately woven into a larger, interconnected tapestry—a tapestry governed by universal laws. These laws are not merely abstract concepts; they are foundational principles that govern the flow of life, the unfolding of the cosmos, and the nature of consciousness itself. They are as immutable and enduring as the forces of gravity or the principles of thermodynamics, yet they are far more subtle in their influence. To understand universal law is to step into a deeper relationship with the universe, that which we have come to know as "God", or whatever you choose to call it, and its mysteries. "God works in mysterious ways", as the saying goes. These laws are not confined to any one religion, culture, or system of thought; they transcend individual human constructs. While interpretations may vary, the core essence of these laws remains constant and operates beyond our limited understanding.

1. The Law of Cause and Effect AKA The Law of Compensation or Karma.

Perhaps the most fundamental of all universal laws is the Law of Cause and Effect, often summed up as "what you sow, you shall reap." This law states that every action, whether it is a thought, word, or deed, creates an effect in the world. Nothing occurs in isolation, and every action reverberates throughout the cosmos, creating ripples that reach far beyond what we can immediately perceive. This law speaks to the interconnectedness of all life. When we act with kindness, we set in motion a chain of positive events that can influence the world in ways we may never fully understand. On the other hand, actions rooted in negativity—be it through hate, greed, or deception—generate their own cycle of cause and effect, often leading to their own undoing. Yet, the Law of Cause and Effect does not merely apply to external actions; it also governs the realm of thoughts and emotions. Our internal state has just as much influence on the universe as our external actions. What we think, feel, and believe influences not only our experience but also the energy we send into the world, creating effects on the energetic plane.

2. The Law of Attraction AKA The Law of Correspondence.

Closely tied to the Law of Cause and Effect is the Law of Attraction. This law suggests that like attracts like. In other words, we draw into our lives that which we focus on, whether consciously or unconsciously. If we focus on abundance, we are more likely to attract opportunities, people, and experiences that align with abundance. Conversely, if we focus on scarcity or fear, we are more likely to attract experiences that reinforce those states. The Law of Attraction operates at the vibrational level, meaning that every thought, word, and action emits a frequency. The universe, through its vast interconnectedness, responds to that frequency by bringing back experiences that match it. This means that our inner reality shapes our outer reality in profound ways. "As within, so without As above so below." Our inner world creates our outer world. However, this law is not as simple as wishing for something and receiving it; it requires alignment between our thoughts, emotions, and actions. True attraction comes from a state of inner harmony, clarity, and trust in the process. When we are aligned with our highest intentions and embody the qualities we wish to attract, we magnetize those things toward us effortlessly.

3. The Law of Rhythm

The Law of Rhythm speaks to the cyclical nature of life. Just as the tides rise and fall, and seasons change from spring to summer to autumn to winter, all things in the universe move in rhythms and cycles. This law reminds us that everything in life has its timing—whether it is a time for growth or a time for rest, a time for creation or a time for destruction. Understanding the Law of Rhythm encourages us to embrace the natural flow of life, trusting that there are seasons for everything. In periods of difficulty or challenge, we can trust that the rhythm of life will eventually shift, bringing new opportunities or moments of clarity. Likewise, during times of prosperity or peace, we are reminded that the cycles of life are ever-moving, and change is inevitable. Recognizing the rhythms within our own lives allows us to work with, rather than against, the natural flow of things. It helps us to know when to push forward with intention and when to surrender to the ebb and flow of the universe or "God".

4.The Law of Polarity

The Law of Polarity, also known as duality, states that everything has its opposite. Light exists because there is darkness, good is understood because of evil, and joy is defined by suffering. This law reflects the dual nature of reality: for every force, there is an equal and opposite force. While it may seem counterintuitive at first, the Law of Polarity reminds us that opposites are not enemies; they are complementary. Without one, the other would not exist. This understanding offers a profound lesson in embracing the full spectrum of life—the light and the dark, the pleasure and the pain, the good and the bad—as all essential parts of the same whole. In times of hardship or suffering, it is vital to remember that polarity works both ways. The moment of greatest struggle often holds the seed for transformation, growth, and a greater understanding of life's deeper purpose. The Law of Polarity invites us to embrace both sides of the coin and see how they contribute to our evolution.

5. The Law of Gender

The Law of Gender asserts that all things have both masculine and feminine energies. These energies exist in balance and harmony within all things, from the natural world to the human experience. Masculine energy is associated with action, structure, and logic, while feminine energy is associated with intuition, receptivity, and creativity. This law reminds us that true creation and progress come not from an imbalance of one energy over the other, but from their cooperation and integration. In every human being, both masculine and feminine energies exist, and when these energies are balanced, an individual can live in greater alignment with their authentic self. The Law of Gender also applies to the broader universe, where creation is not solely an act of will or force, but also a process of receptivity and nurturing. The ebb and flow of these energies are essential to the ongoing dance of life.

6. The Law of Divine Oneness

The Law of Divine Oneness encompasses the profound truth that everything in the universe is interconnected. Every thought, action, and event is part of a vast, unified whole. This law reflects the deep truth that the separation we perceive between ourselves and others is an illusion. We are all expressions of the same source energy, and at a fundamental level, we are all one. When we understand this law, we begin to live with a greater sense of compassion and empathy, recognizing that harming another is, in essence, harming ourselves. The energy we put into the world is felt by all beings, and the collective consciousness is shaped by every individual thought and action. Living in accordance with the Law of Divine Oneness means recognizing the divine within everything—the interconnectedness of all life—and cultivating a deep reverence for the sacred nature of existence. It asks us to expand our view of reality, seeing not just our own lives, but the lives of all beings, as part of a vast, divine expression. Namaste, as the saying goes, means the divine light within me recognizes and honors the divine light within you. We are one body, one mind, one consciousness.

7. The Law of Perpetual Transmutation of Energy

The Law of Perpetual Transmutation of Energy asserts that energy is always in motion and constantly changing form. Nothing is static; everything is in a continuous state of transformation. This law teaches us that we, too, have the ability to transmute the energy around us. Through conscious intention, we can change negative energy into positive energy, fear into love, or chaos into clarity. This is alchemy; using the power of love to transmute a negative to a positive to create miracles. Alchemy is taking the lessons and experience from life and turning it into knowledge and wisdom; taking your pain and turning it into power and purpose. LEAD INTO GOLD. Understanding this law empowers us to take control of our own energy field. When we encounter challenges or negative circumstances, we have the capacity to shift the energy through our thoughts, actions, and vibrations. The universe responds to the energy we emit, and by transmuting it, we can manifest new possibilities and realities.

Universal law is not merely a philosophical concept; it is the underlying framework of existence itself.

Understanding and aligning with these laws enables us to live with greater harmony, purpose, and clarity. Just as we learn to navigate the physical laws of nature—gravity, motion, and energy—we can learn to navigate the spiritual laws that govern the unseen realms of consciousness and existence. In embracing universal law, we take our place as conscious creators in the grand dance of life. And as we do so, we unlock the potential to create lives of greater meaning, fulfillment, and connection—lives that resonate in harmony with the profound laws that guide the universe.

Now let's talk about consciousness and the 7 chakras real quick.

What are the 7 chakras? They are the 7 energy centers of the body to put it short. The seven main chakras, in order, are the Root, Sacral, Solar Plexus, Heart, Throat, Third Eye, and Crown. Each chakra is associated with specific aspects of our physical, emotional, and spiritual well-being.

1. Root Chakra (Muladhara): Located at the base of the spine, it governs survival, security, and stability. It is associated with grounding, physical health, and basic needs. A balanced root chakra provides a strong foundation for life. This is where most people tend to store their energy closing off their heart keeping them in fear and survival

2. Sacral Chakra (Svadhisthana): Situated below the navel, it deals with emotions, creativity, and sexuality. It influences personal relationships, pleasure, and emotional expression. A balanced sacral chakra promotes joy and emotional well-being.

3. Solar Plexus Chakra (Manipura): Located in the upper abdomen, it governs confidence, self-esteem, and personal power. It is associated with willpower, ambition, and self-efficacy. A balanced solar plexus chakra allows one to assert their place in the world.

4. Heart Chakra (Anahata): Situated in the center of the chest, it deals with love, compassion, and connection. It is associated with empathy, forgiveness, and emotional healing. A balanced heart chakra facilitates open and loving relationships.

5. Throat Chakra (Vishuddha): Located in the throat area, it governs communication, self-expression, and authenticity. It is associated with clear and honest communication, and expressing one's true self. A balanced throat chakra allows for confident and assertive communication.

6. Third Eye Chakra (Ajna) aka the Pineal Gland: Situated between the eyebrows, it governs intuition, insight, and clarity. It is associated with psychic abilities, wisdom, and spiritual awareness. A balanced third eye chakra enhances discernment. It is the sixth sense of intuition your eye into the spiritual realms and the eye the Hebrew Bible refers to saying "If thine eye be single your whole body will be full of light". It is also heavily targeted with toxins such as fluoride, a neurotoxin, which calcifies the gland closing us off spiritually.

7. Crown Chakra (Sahasrara): Located at the top of the head, it governs spirituality, connection to higher consciousness, and enlightenment. It is associated with wisdom, enlightenment, and a connection to the divine. A balanced crown chakra facilitates a sense of unity and purpose.

Now Consciousness:

Consciousness is all that is.

Consciousness is pure creative CONSCIOUS energy.

It is the very thing that gives you life and your awareness according to the level you are on.

There are 7 states of consciousness:

- Waking
- Sleeping
- Dreaming
- Transcendental
- Cosmic
- God &
- Unity Consciousness
- Together they make the 8th which is Brahman the WHOLE

These describe levels of consciousness or reality even further:

3D (Third Dimension) – Physical reality; duality, ego, linear thinking, materialism, fear based narrative, survival...

4D (Fourth Dimension) – The bridge between physical and spiritual; includes time, intuition, dreams, awakening...

5D (Fifth Dimension) – Unity consciousness; unconditional love, compassion, manifestation, oneness, abundance...

6D and higher – Higher states of consciousness, divine knowledge, soul-level awareness, multidimensional beings...

Each higher dimension is said to hold more light, frequency, and divine awareness.

The entire purpose of the human experience is the expansion of consciousness, for all life to learn, GROW, expand and EVOLVE.

As we grow and develop spiritually we naturally ascend to higher levels of consciousness as our awareness expands or transcendental meditation is a great proven practical technique to release stress, regulate the nervous system and reach higher levels more intentionally.

Of course there is a lot more to this so as always:

💥Disclaimer 💥

I always encourage everyone to do their own research and form their own beliefs. Your beliefs are POWERFUL they create your reality. Take what resonates and leave the rest. If your beliefs are serving you well, if you are creating and living a life that you love or moving towards it, more power to you😉 If not you've got to take a look at your mindset.

Personally I know it is my mission and purpose to SHIFT the consciousness of humanity at this time as more souls are awakening to higher divine infinite universal TRUTH.

We are shifting into Unity Consciousness aka Christ Consciousness where we realize we are all one body, one mind, one consciousness expressing itself in a multitude of fashions but all still expressions of the one infinite source.

One source or so called "God".

Multiple temples or vessels to experience life and all that is.

It is infinite eternal omnipresent and omnipotent.

It always is, always was and always will be.

I had this aha moment the other day...Some people argue that the entire Bible is an allegory. I know it is loaded with metaphors and parables.

I thought, what if Jesus calming the storm of the ocean, was a metaphor for transcendental consciousness and our ability to access our own inner peace to calm the storms?

As I student at MIU for Consciousness and Human Potential I practice transcendental meditation every day.

We use the metaphor of the ocean and basically it goes like this:

Life is found in layers. All of life is one vast ocean of consciousness pure creative CONSCIOUS energy – the Quantum Field.

At the top of the ocean are the waves the storms the challenges and chaos of life and the good thoughts it all manifests here at the surface level. This is us and our every day experience in waking consciousness.

Below that we go deeper and deeper into the levels of who we truly are until we get to the depths of the ocean where a peace and stillness naturally exists. Be still and know. This is the unified field the source of all thought and creation.

It is our true essence the I AM.

It's there WITHIN us and always has been for us to access. It's who we are at our core. I AM love. I AM light. I am that I AM. In Vedic traditions they say "I am That".

Transcendental meditation is a proven practical technique to achieve transcendental consciousness and essentially plug in to our source to recharge.

It effortlessly releases stress, regulates the nervous system and gives you more rest relaxation and rejuvenation in 20 minutes than in a whole night's sleep.

The more you practice it the more you begin to bring the qualities of infinite unbounded consciousness out into your waking day allowing you to be more calm, peaceful, centered and balanced able to respond with Love instead of reacting in every day life. This state is known as Cosmic Consciousness.

It is actually PROVEN that groups of meditators lower crime rates, health improves, wars have stopped and many other statistics showing improvement.

It is calculated that it would only take an estimated 10% of the population meditating to essentially create world peace. This is known as they Maharishi Effect. To learn more about this please visit TM.org.

So, yes, life is found in layers and we must peel them away like the layers of an onion to get to the TRUTH of who we are! In psychology, models of human development, this concept is known as "unfreezing", where we unlearn previous beliefs so we can relearn to level up in consciousness and life. You can't solve a problem with the same level of consciousness you used to create it. You must RISE ABOVE IT.

There are 16 Principles of Creative Intelligence that I find so profound and would love to share with you all as well. They can be used as a guide in life regardless of your current beliefs or religion.

1. The Nature of Life is to GROW
2. Divine Order is Present Everywhere
3. Life is Found in Layers
4. Outer Depends on Inner
5. Seek the Highest First
6. Rest & Activity Are the Steps to Progress
7. Enjoy Greater Efficacy & Accomplish More
8. Every Action Has a Reaction
9. Purification Leads to Progress
10. The Field of All Possibilities is the Source of All Solutions
11. Thoughts Lead to Action Action Leads to Achievement & Achievement Leads to Fulfillment
12. Knowledge is Gained from Both Outside & Inside
13. Knowledge is Structured in Consciousness
14. Harmony Exists in Diversity
15. The Whole is Contained in Every Part
16. The Whole is Greater Than the Sum of the Parts

CHAPTER 5

Mindset Creates Reality

Everyone is creating their own reality. It is a matter of whether you are a conscious, deliberate creator or you're just living life unconsciously on autopilot. Either you want to change your life OR you don't. You simply have to make up your MIND. You see, your mindset is creating your reality. Mindset is a collection of your beliefs; what you believe to be true about yourself, others and the world. What you believe to be true, hold in your mind and heart and take action upon consistently will manifest into physical tangible reality sooner or later. You reap what you sow in the garden of your mind.

The problem with this is we have been programmed all wrong. Our minds are super computers wired with beliefs, thoughts, feelings and perceptions that we filter all the information in our reality through using our five senses. We see the world not as it is but as we are. We have been experiencing life based on old outdated programs that are no longer serving us. Our minds need an upgrade, new better apps and updated software so we, the hardware of the system can run optimally as the best version of ourselves. If we want to reach more of our potential we must shift our mindset.

This can be a simple process. Notice I said simple, not EASY. If it was easy everyone would do it. We say we want change but change is hard. We are creatures of habit and change requires us to unwire and rewire these subconscious or unconscious programs that we have been running off of. First we must peel away the layers of everything we've been taught to believe and have accepted as truth. This is usually referred to as a spiritual awakening, personal development, spiritual growth, shadow work etc.

Your mindset consists of conditioned beliefs from childhood, religion, past experiences including those related to trauma, cultural, family and societal beliefs etc. What we come into agreement with becomes part of our belief system. We believe it to be true and so it is. Your beliefs will be different depending on all of these things.

A belief is simply a thought that we continue to think. Every time we think a thought we are firing and wiring synapses or electrical circuits in the brain that connect over and over and eventually they solidify creating learned programs of information. It's how we learn everything and why "practice makes perfect". The more you think a thought or perform an action the more it becomes a natural reoccurring habit or pattern that we perform without much conscious effort on our part.

Just like riding a bike or driving a car is difficult at first but then becomes second nature, so is the process for all new habits and learned behavior. This is why change is hard.

All creation starts in the mind. We have 60-70,000 thoughts per day and 90% of those thoughts are the same on repeat every single day. Majority of people are programmed where they wake up and start thinking about their problems, blaming, shaming and complaining. These are difficult patterns to break and it all starts with your mindset.

Let's talk really quick about victim mindset vs growth mindset. We can either be in a problem structure or a creative structure. Victim mindset is fear, blame and survival in the problem structure where we are focused on everything that is wrong in our lives and we tend to complain a lot. We say "why is this happening to me?" whereas with a growth mindset we ask ourselves "what is this trying to teach me?". A growth mindset can propel us forward and a victim mindset will keep us stuck creating the very things we say we don't want. With a growth mindset we focus our time, energy and attention on what we do want, a higher vision for our lives and possible solutions as we take action to move towards it.

People with a growth mindset tend to be more focused on gratitude and what they do have instead on what they do not. This is known as the Matthew Effect, coming from the book of Matthew in the Hebrew Bible. It says, "Those who are grateful will be given in abundance and those who are not grateful, even what they have will be taken from them." You don't know what you have until it's gone.

So since our mindset is playing such a huge role in the creation of our reality, we must first become aware that change is necessary and the fact that change must begin within ourselves. It is not some outside factor that is going to magically save us from ourselves. Once we are aware and willing to take radical responsibility for our own free will and choice and the power we hold to create with our mindset, we can get to work doing the inner work that is needed to shift what we are experiencing in the outer world. This is sometimes called shadow work and something we all come here to do at some point. I always say "To each their own path. Ultimately all paths lead WITHIN where the real work must be done." I have come across many techniques to help with this and I personally use the Five Steps to Conscious Creation which I will go into in another chapter. For now, just know that the good news is your beliefs can change. You can change your mind and changing your mind can change your life.

We are even told in the Bible that mindset creates reality. Jesus said "as a man thinkith so shall he become" and "as you believe in your heart so shall it be done until you". This implies that thoughts and emotions play a part in the creation of our reality.

Buddha said "What we imagine we create. What we feel we attract. What we think we become."

Napoleon Hill author of Think and Grow Rich said, "Whatever the mind can conceive and believe it can achieve."

Thoughts become things. Everything is created twice. Once in the mind and second in physical reality- material manifestation.

Creative source energy or "God" works through us. We are the bridge between the spiritual and physical realms. We are the hands and feet so to speak. We are not separate from this creative energy. It is part of us and we are part of it- One body, one MIND, one consciousness expressing itself in multiple forms. We each create our own individual reality and we co create a collective story or narrative of our world as a whole. We can choose to take control of our mindset, SHIFT it and create a whole new reality right here, right now, on this old earth that is passing and becoming anew- We are Awakening & Making the Shift into the Quantum New 5D Earth Paradigm- Heaven on Earth.

🔆 Disclaimer 🔆

I always encourage everyone to do their own research and form their own beliefs. Your beliefs are POWERFUL they create your reality. Take what resonates and leave the rest. If your beliefs are serving you well, if you are creating and living a life that you love or moving towards it, more power to you☺ If not you've got to take a look at your mindset.

CHAPTER 6

The Five Steps to Conscious Creation

So, now that we are beginning to understand how our own thoughts, feelings, energy and emotions, which are energy in motion, play a part in the creation of our reality, how do we bring them all into alignment with our calling and purpose?

Well, first we must define what it means to live our true nature and purpose. To me our true nature is a pure creative spirit and our purpose is to express that creativity in the most authentic way possible. We are each individual waves of consciousness or children of God, special and unique. Our purpose is ultimately to share our experience, knowledge, wisdom, talents and gifts with the world to be of service. Choosing to live your true nature and purpose is one of the core four choices of the Magnetic Mind Method which I am certified in. Let's discuss the core four choices and what a true choice is.

We are beings of free will and choice and as such we get to choose what we create. The premise of the Magnetic Mind Method is that we are not broken and we do not need to be fixed. We are powerful creators and we get to choose what we create. To be in a creative structure in full creation mode creating from our hearts, tapped into our intuition, creating from God consciousness, instead of from ego, we want to choose the core four choices everyday. We already know "I choose the end result of living my true nature and purpose". In no particular order we also choose the end result of living a life that we love, having health and vitality and being the predominant creative force in our lives. Being the predominant creative force means that we understand we are creating our own reality. Our thoughts, feelings, emotions, intentions and actions compound. We aren't victims. We are creators and with this awareness we can create with intention and purpose, focusing our time, energy and attention on what we want to see manifest. We focus on a higher vision or mission and take aligned action instead of blaming, shaming or making excuses. I choose the end result of living a life that I love. Get really clear on what that means to you without limitations. Anything is possible. I choose the end result of health and vitality and what that would look like in your life. You decide what you want in these areas. You choose them everyday and take aligned actions towards it. Remember, what you do not change, YOU ARE CHOOSING.

So to recap the core four choices are:

1. I choose the end result of being the predominant creative force in my life.
2. I choose the end result of living a life that I love.
3. I choose the end result of health and vitality.
4. I choose the end result of living my true nature and purpose.

Once you release resistance to these core four choices and can live them in the now, you are then in a creative structure and can create more of what you love. True choices are things you choose simply because you would love to have them, like living in your dream home or creating a successful E.L.F. business. E.L.F. is an acronym for easy, lucrative and fun. Resistance is what holds us back from taking action towards our goals. Resistance is all the reasons and stories we tell ourselves as to why we can't do or have something. The six self sabotaging beliefs majority struggle with for example:

1. I'm not enough
2. I'm not worthy
3. I'm not capable
4. I'm insignificant
5. I don't belong
6. I'm not perfect

These are lies not based on love and TRUTH. You are worthy, more than enough, significant, you are capable, you belong, and you are perfect as you are because you ARE. I AM perfect as I am because I AM. We've been programmed based on lies and deceptions meant to manipulate human consciousness by taking control of our minds. We have been living in the dark but we are the light of the world. We have been Dumbed Down, Drugged Up and Disempowered- but we are Awakening and Making the Shift into the Quantum New 5D Earth Paradigm.

So the five steps to conscious creation. Step one, we choose. I choose the end result of living a life that I love. You choose it and you step into it as if it were already done.

BTW this isn't just "whoo whoo" spirituality, hippie stuff. This is neuroplasticity, the rewiring of the brain. Neuroscience and epigenetics is revolutionizing the field of psychology and what we previously thought was possible as far as human potential. We used to think things just run in the family and that we can't change our genes or genetic code. Truth is we are the writers of the code and epigenetics proves that our cells change shape and form according to what we believe, think, feel and speak. We can signal our genes before our environment to create a new reality from the inside out by using our imagination. Albert Einstein said, "Imagination is everything. It is a preview of life's coming attractions." He also said that, "The best way to predict the future is to create it." We can remove generational curses, limitations, and recode our DNA to reach higher levels of potential. We do this by tapping into the innate divine wisdom and intelligence that is within us and changing the information. Our entire existence is because of this divine innate wisdom, intelligence, higher power, God if you will, and we are not separate from it but connected to it. As such we are creating with every word that we speak and thought that we hold with intention consistently and take action upon. We are creating it all, we just haven't been aware of it. Awaken oh yee sleeper and RISE UP!

So we imagine what it would be like to live a life that we love. What would it feel like? What would you be doing? Who would you be with? See yourself in your mind's eye. Feel it in your heart. This creates brain and heart coherence or ALIGNMENT. A clear intention combined with an elevated emotion such as gratitude "it's already done", begins to rewire the brain and create new neurological pathways that allow the mind and body to work together instead of against one another.

So this choice feels really amazing but you hear those voices trying to creep in already telling you why you can't have it. This brings us to step 3, creating structural tension. A structure is anything with two or more points that work together. In this case the structure is where you are and where you want to be. So we want to bring up the gap. To do this we ask ourselves, okay so I'm choosing to live a life that I love but I can't because...Because why??? At this point all the resistance and limiting beliefs will begin to surface. All the excuses and stories. While they feel very real and you did experience these things at some point and time, if we keep telling the same stories we keep our energy stuck in the past, creating from an egoic structure. "We can't create a new future stuck in a familiar past". "Your mind can either be a record of the past or a MAP to the future"- Dr Joe Dispenza. We will keep recreating past experiences until we get the lesson and clear our karma. Nonetheless everything will begin to come up.

I'm not worthy, I'm not enough, I'm not capable, I'm insignificant, I don't belong, I'm not perfect, I don't have the time, I don't have the money, I don't have the skills, talent, it can't happen for me, others can do it but not me, they must have something that I don't, you don't know what I've been through... etc etc etc.

Now that we are shining the light on these lies we can transmute or alchemize them. Alchemy uses the power of love to change a negative experience into a positive one so you can get the lesson and move forward- turn your pain into power and purpose; your experience into knowledge and wisdom. We rate the resistance on a scale of 1-10, then this brings us to step #4.

Superconscious Transformation Recode. The recode is the fourth step in the 5 steps to conscious creation. It's the rewiring of old outdated mental programming, self sabotaging, limiting beliefs and any conditioned information learned through past experience or trauma. Superconscious is your third level of memory or mind, I'll talk about in a second. Ego is the first and it is formed in the first 7 years of life; all the programmed information you accumulate based on where you are born, cultural, societal, family, religious beliefs etc...

Second is your subconscious/unconscious mind which by the time we are 35 years old 90% of what we do is based on our subconscious programming. The Hebrew Bible says, "Be not conformed to the ways of the world but be transformed by the renewing of your mind." We are running off of conditioned programs and beliefs that serve a fear based narrative in which only a select few hold the power and control even though we are all sovereign free beings. Dr. Carl Jung the well known psychologist said, "Until the unconscious becomes conscious, it will rule your life and man will call it fate." Jesus said, "forgive them father for they know not what they do" and Dr. Joseph Murphy author of The Power of the Subconscious Mind said, "Ignorance is the only sin and suffering is the consequence".

Outside of these programs and unconscious beliefs that create our reality is the Superconscious level of memory "the book of life". This level of memory holds all information throughout all time and space from this lifetime and past lifetimes. Again, we are energy, spirit, soul and that part of us is infinite and eternal, it doesn't die, it TRANSFORMS. "Energy is neither created nor destroyed" -Albert Einstein.

The Superconscious field of memory holds all information from your soul's inception, until now. Every thought, word, deed, emotion, act, experience etc. is held in this field of information; the quantum or unified field. Some may call it "the book of life" or the akashic records.

With your permission I intuitively go through the process of rewiring, recoding, clearing your energy centers (chakras), shifting identities, activating and upgrading DNA and mind on all levels. This helps you begin to release the resistance and create new empowering beliefs that are in alignment with universal absolute TRUTH, which is LOVE, your true divine spiritual nature and the essence of your BEing. Love is the highest TRUTH. Love is a frequency or vibration- the highest in the YOUniverse.

I go through emotions, raise your vibration, break generational curses, soul ties or agreements and cut energetic cords that are draining your energy. I allow the Superconscious to rewire itself accordingly, trusting that it will lead us on the path of least resistance where we will flow towards our desired end result. When it feels good, like things have shifted and resistance is gone we ground and come back to the present moment.

It's a beautiful, POWERFUL, laid back process that you can even do for yourself because in truth you have the same power and potential. It's just nice to have someone walk you through it.

Now that you have let go and integrated the resistance you will feel lighter, ready to take on step 5. The fifth and final step to conscious creation is to take the aligned action. Now that you have shifted your beliefs, your mind, your emotions etc you are in alignment and can go out and take the action in the physical world to make your dreams a reality. "Faith without works is dead". We must take action steps little by little to create in this world. It's a process and we must trust it. Stick with it and be consistent. The journey of 1000 miles starts with one step! Rome wasn't built in a day and the day we plant the seed isn't the day we eat the fruit. There is a process to creation. A method to the madness. It's taken us years, decades, lifetimes to get to this point. It will take some time to unlearn and relearn; to unwire and rewire. This five step process is a simple easy effective way to compound actions, create massive momentum and take quantum leaps in our own personal/spiritual development, journey, transformation and ultimately in our EVOLution. If you're interested in learning more or experiencing this process for yourself, I'll give you all the details for that in the last chapter and on the information page. For now, let's move on to why speaking your TRUTH is your SUPERPOWER.

CHAPTER 7

Your Truth Your Story & Your Message Matter

In a world filled with noise, distractions, and constant opinions, it can be easy to lose sight of what matters most: your truth, your story, and your message. We often find ourselves looking outward for validation, trying to align with someone else's narrative, or fitting into molds that society has set for us. But there is an inherent power in owning your personal truth, telling your own story, and sharing your unique message with the world.

The Power of Your Truth

Your truth is your foundation. It's the unfiltered, unapologetic essence of who you are. It's what drives your actions, shapes your thoughts, and defines your experiences. So often, we shy away from our truth, either because we fear judgment or because we feel it doesn't fit the expectations set by others. But the reality is, your truth is sacred. It is the only thing that can never be taken away from you.

Embracing your truth means accepting your flaws and celebrating your victories. It means understanding that who you are- every bit of your imperfections and strengths- is valuable. Your truth doesn't have to be polished or perfect; it just has to be real. When you embrace your truth, you give yourself permission to show up as your authentic self. And when you show up authentically, others are inspired to do the same. One of my mantras has been "I desire to attract thee most badass spiritually alive souls into my businesses to create real and lasting change in our lives and aspire to inspire others to do the same."

The world is starving for truth. People are tired of the curated, filtered versions of reality that we see on social media or the "perfect lives" that seem to surround us. What resonates deeply with people is realness. Your truth, no matter how raw, messy, or difficult it may seem, is what connects you to others on a deeper level. When you speak from your heart, you open doors to meaningful connections and create a space for others to reflect on their own truths.

The Impact of Your Story

Your story is the map that leads you to where you are today. It's filled with the moments of growth, challenges, triumphs, and even failures that have shaped you. Every twist and turn has contributed to the person you have become. Your story isn't just for you, it's for others too. It's a gift.

When you share your story, you offer the world a mirror to reflect in. Your experiences, struggles, and successes can serve as a guide for someone else who might be walking a similar path. We are all interconnected, and the experiences you've lived through may hold the key to someone else's breakthrough. When you allow yourself to be vulnerable enough to share your narrative, you empower others to do the same. In that shared vulnerability, there is strength, courage, and connection.

Perhaps you've faced hardship that you now see as a lesson. Maybe you've been through challenges that, at one point, seemed insurmountable. When you share these parts of your life, you show others that there is hope, there is resilience, and there is always the potential for transformation. Your story becomes a beacon of light in the darkness for someone who might be struggling with their own battles.

But it's not just about the struggles. Your story includes your victories, your breakthroughs, and the times when you overcame the odds. Those moments are just as powerful because they show that change is possible, that growth is real, and that there is always more to come. Your story is proof that no matter where you start, you have the ability to rewrite the ending.

The Importance of Your Message

Your message is what you want the world to know. It's the core lesson, insight, or truth that you are meant to share with others. It's what you believe can make a difference, and it's what compels you to speak, to create, to take action.

Each person has a unique message that only they can share. It's the seed of inspiration that can spark change in others, the idea that can challenge someone's perspective, or the encouragement that can help someone persevere. But often, we hesitate to voice our message because we fear it won't be well received or that it isn't important enough. But in truth, your message matters more than you might think.

The world needs your voice. The world needs the wisdom that only you can impart. The messages we need to hear often come from the most unexpected sources, and that's because everyone has a perspective that can enrich the collective understanding. When you hold back your message, you not only deprive yourself of the opportunity to impact others, but you also deny the world the possibility of growth through your insights.

You might wonder, "What difference does my message make?" But think about it this way: A single spark can ignite a fire. A single thought, when shared, can inspire a revolution. History is full of individuals whose messages, often simple yet profound, changed the course of events. It wasn't always the loudest voice or the most polished speech, it was the truth that resonated deeply with people.

Your message doesn't have to be grand or revolutionary to matter. It simply needs to be true to who you are and what you stand for. When you speak your truth with conviction, when you share your story honestly, and when you deliver your message with love and authenticity, you create ripples in the collective consciousness. Those ripples can spread further than you ever imagined.

Why It All Matters

In the end, your truth, your story, and your message are all intertwined. They are the truest expression of who you are and why you matter. They give you a platform to make an impact, not only on your own life but on the lives of others.

When you honor your truth, you find peace and clarity within yourself. When you share your story, you connect with others on a deep human level. And when you deliver your message, you contribute to the world in a way that only you can. Every person's journey is different, but the power of sharing your truth, telling your story, and spreading your message transcends individual experiences, it becomes part of a collective movement of change, growth, and healing.

Remember, you don't need to wait for permission to live out your truth. You don't need to wait for the perfect moment to share your story. The world is ready for your message, even if you're still unsure about how it will be received. The most important thing is to begin. Your truth, your story, and your message matter because you matter. And the world needs what only you can offer. Your mess can become your message and your story is your power. Live your truth unapologetically as the most authentic version of yourself. Follow your unique path, trust the process and enjoy the journey. You are meant for greatness.

CHAPTER 8

I AM Soul EVOLution - Awaken the Creator Within- How to Use All This to Create Transformation in Ourselves & the World

So, now that we are beginning to understand how our thoughts, feelings, & actions are playing such a huge part in the creation of our reality, what does this mean for our future? Well, Albert Einstein said, "The best way to predict the future is to create it". Since we are beginning to understand that everything is actually energy and that what we focus on, give our time, energy and attention to, we are creating, we can begin to make the shift. Neville Goddard says in his book Manifesting Miracles that the secret to creating miracles is to shift your attention from what you don't want to what you do want. Where we place our attention is where we place our energy and what we focus on expands. Where focus goes, energy FLOWS. What we place our attention on GROWS.

Showing love, appreciation and gratitude for where we are opens the door to allow more blessings to flow. Practicing gratitude is one habit of highly successful people. A few more to remember are SAVERS. Silence Affirmations Visualization Exercise Reading and Scribing. Taking time to set intentions, create goals and plan out your week for success is also a great habit to develop.

Silence – I enjoy doing my transcendental meditation.

Affirmations – I read my MAP my Miracle Action Plan to rewire my mind so I attract my desires and I listen to my morning routine playlist with a variety of gratitude affirmations and motivational favorites. You can get your FREE Miracle Action Plan PDF on my link

Visualization – I visualize and imagine my desires as if they are already done.

Exercise – I like Qi Gong which combines stretching, energy and breath work.

Reading – Audio books are my jam. You can listen on the go.

Scribing – Journaling, writing out gratitude, intentions and goals.

I also choose the core four choices every day to be in a creative structure and I do a quick recode.

Create and develop a morning routine that works for you and gets you in a strong, powerful mindset ready to take on your day.

Rest and activity are the steps to progress. We can be more effective in life and accomplish more by doing less when we understand this. 80/20 principle. 20% of your efforts will equal 80% of your results. We aren't meant to constantly be on the go go go. Resting and taking action from a place of power and alignment is way more efficient. Instead of being matter trying to force matter and make things happen, we make SHIFT happen. Inner energetic shifts in our mindset will create shifts in our outer reality. When we are in this space of surrender and allowing we begin to attract the right people, opportunities and circumstances. It's still up to us to take the aligned action and follow our calling. We must be bold and courageous enough to not only speak our truth but to live it.

Moving forward and creating change and transformation won't always be easy. It takes commitment and a really strong will to continue on the path of personal development and spiritual growth. It's going to take conscious effort and energy to create new habits and patterns of thinking, being and doing that are in alignment with this new version of yourself.

How I do this is by using the Five Steps to Conscious Creation which we discussed in chapter 6. We can simply decide or choose what we want, create the vision or goal and go for it. The only thing standing in our way is ourselves; our own fear and doubt. The limiting beliefs and emotions from past experiences will try to keep us locked in old identities trapped, recreating a predictable future based on a familiar past. Again, Albert Einstein said the best way to predict the future is to create it. Remember our personality creates our personal reality. The way we think, feel and act every day creates our life experience.

So just to recap the 5 Steps to Conscious Creation:

Step 1- Create the vision. Decide what you want without limitations. All things are possible. We have access to limitless potential and infinite possibilities for our lives, we simply have to choose.

Step 2- Imagine this new future reality as if it were already done. Feel the emotions you would feel. Feeling is the secret. We want our mind and body working together. Brain and heart coherence. Using our imagination is powerful. It's how we create. What we envision in our mind and hold in our hearts we inevitably create. Again, I quote Albert Einstein who said, "Imagination is everything. It is a preview of life's coming attractions." Using our imagination actually triggers our cells to change structure and so we can trigger them ahead of our environment to create change from the inside out. This is the science of epigenetics, which tells us that our thoughts and feelings affect us on a cellular level.

Step 3- We create structural tension. This means we create two points. Where you are and where you want to be. How do we do that? Simple. We ask okay well I'm choosing to live a life that I love but I can't because... this creates the two points, where you are and where you want to be. Everything that is in the way will start to come up to the surface in the gap. I choose to live a life that I love but I can't because... I'm not enough, I'm not worthy, I'm not capable, I'm insignificant, I don't belong, I'm not perfect, I don't have the time, I don't have the money, you don't know what I've been through, this person, look at how bad the world is and the list goes on and on. Asking this question creates the structure and triggers all the resistance into the field.

Step 4- Step 4 is the recode. Superconscious Transformation Recode. We have 3 levels of memory or mind. The ego formed in the first 7 years of life, the subconscious mind which by the time we are 35 years old 90% of what we do is based on this unconscious programming, habits and patterns, and outside of that is the Superconscious level of memory which is infinite and eternal. It holds all information throughout all time and space from your soul's inception until now. I mentioned it earlier. It's the book of life. We have the power and potential to rewire the information in our memory so we can release the beliefs, trauma and emotions that are no longer serving us and we can recode or rewrite our DNA to reach higher levels of potential. DNA is simply encrypted information. Information can be changed, updated and reprocessed.

The field of neuroscience and epigenetics is revolutionizing psychology and what we previously thought was possible as far as the power of our minds. We also previously thought genes were set in stone. Epigenetics now tells us we are the writers of the code. We can change the information through our own intention. The process is very laid back and only takes a few minutes. It activates the mind's own innate power and divine intelligence to release and melt away the resistance that has been holding us back from the **5th and FINAL STEP** which is **ALIGNED ACTION.**

So you see, it's simple really. We decide what we want and we go for it. We remove what's in the way and take powerful, purposeful aligned action towards our vision and goals. We create change and transformation in the world first and foremost by creating change and transformation within our own selves. We focus our time, energy and attention on being the best version of ourselves and shining our light to help illuminate the path for others by sharing your own authentic experience, story, message and gifts with the world.

So, maybe you don't know what those are yet or how to get started. This is what I help people do. I help you ditch toxins from your home, mind, body and spirit and get out of your own way so you can create a life you love and impact those around you along the way. This is how we create change, total wellness and transformation in ourselves and the world. We must own our personal power, take back our sovereignty and take radical responsibility for our own free will and choice. If you are interested in learning more about potentially working with me, all of my information will be available here in the book.

There is a radical shift taking place. A Paradigm shift that the world so desperately needs. Fear to love. Ego to soul. Lack and scarcity into abundance and prosperity which is our true divine birthright. Separation and division into unity. We are all spiritual beings here on this earth having a human experience. We come here to experience life, learn, grow, expand and EVOLve. Love is truly the answer. Love is the highest TRUTH. Everything else has been an illusion. We have been Dumbed Down, Drugged Up and Disempowered- but we are Awakening and Making the Shift into the Quantum New 5D Earth Paradigm. The New Earth is about moving back to more holistic ways of life. Homebirth, homeschool, work from home and homesteading. We are moving out of the old systems of control; the systems of darkness that have kept us in bondage. Now that we know the TRUTH we can be set FREE. We must be the change we wish to see. Remember, the secret to change isn't to focus our energy on fighting the old but on CREATING the new because we are creators and where focus goes energy flows. What we focus on EXPANDS. SHIFT your identity, your energy, your attention, your FREQUENCY to align with the Quantum New 5D Earth Paradigm- Love & Truth- where magic and miracles are an every day part of life. The time is NOW. Make SHIFT Happen. Let's GROW.

As a student at MIU – Maharishi International University – for my bachelor's in Consciousness and Human Potential I recently had a project in my course "Who AM I". We had to create a map first of our life thus far since birth and then a map of our future. My map shows the evolution in consciousness and the revolutionary paradigm shift that is taking place. It's not he greatest work of art with my stick figures lol but I did get an A! I hope it will give you a visual of it all to understand on a deeper level.

My first MAP showed me being born and my flow through life which included many highs and lows, traumatic events and some huge milestones with lots of lessons along the way. This shows that we are, in truth, not our past but we are who we CHOOSE to become! We cannot create a new future stuck in a familiar past. Our mind can either be a record of the past, or a MAP to the future! What will YOU choose?

You've just completed Dumbed Down, Drugged Up, and Disempowered, Awakening, and Making the Shift into the New Quantum 5D Earth Paradigm. That's no small feat, it means you're ready for real transformation.

The insights you've gained are powerful, but knowledge alone doesn't create change. Integration does. Embodiment does. Aligned action does because "faith without works is dead".

If you're ready to take the next step and turn awareness into lasting transformation, I invite you to visit my page https://linktr.ee/miraclemaven?subscribe

Here you'll find a range of services designed to support your continued awakening, healing, and empowerment including Holistic Health and Wellness Products, Quantum Healing Technology and State of the Art Magnetic Mind Coaching for Total Wellness and Transformation Mind Body & Spirit~

You can also connect with me directly through the site. Let's explore what path forward best supports you in living fully aligned with your highest truth & greatest potential.

The shift has begun. Now let's make it real. Together we can create the New Earth. Can't wait to connect on the other side in QuantumMemberSHIFT.space

Make Shift Happen. Let's GROW.

About the Author

I'm Andrea 😄 the Magnetic Mompreneur 🧲

Quantum Manifestation Coach Spiritual Mindset Mentor & Holistic Wellness Advocate

I am a 39-year-old breastfeeding, home birthing, unschooling mompreneur of 4 from Pennsylvania.

I am an International and Amazon best-selling author of the collaborative book Dream Big Do Bigger Build the Bridge Between Your Dreams and Reality 🌉🧲

I share content on mindset, spirituality, personal development, entrepreneurship, homebirth, unschooling, consciousness, online business & more.

I am completely obsessed with human transformation and the process of creation, and I AM on a mission to SHIFT the consciousness of humanity 🧘‍♀️🌱🦋

If you're on a holistic health and wellness, spiritual awakening journey...

YOU'RE IN THE RIGHT PLACE

There is a REVOLUTION upon us and you may be hearing the call to fulfill a higher purpose, be of service and create CHANGE in the world.

I got the call many years ago and have been following my passion and living my purpose ever since.

Now I am here to help guide others.

I am a superconscious creator & transformation accelerator. I help you awaken to your divine soul truth, find your purpose & take your power back. I help momprenuers & spiritual entrepreneurs specifically, to overcome limited programming & make their dreams reality Making Dreams Reality.

I can help you ditch toxins from your home, mind, body and spirit AFFORDABLY to heal, transform, and create a life that you love

Making the Shift Magick Miracles & Alchemy Quantum Manifestation Coaching
Spiritual Mindset &
Holistic Wellness
Making Dreams Reality

In January 2020 I made the decision to become a coach and since then I've studied all things mindset and spirituality and I've become a Transformational Master Quantum Manifestation Coach Spiritual Mindset Mentor Intuitive Healer & Akashic Records Practitioner certified in Nuerolinguistic Programming Emotional Freedom Tapping & Time Techniques Life & Success Coaching as well as Hypnotherapy & the Magnetic Mind Method. I'm also currently attending Maharishi International University for my bachelor's in consciousness and human potential

As a Certified Magnetic Mind Coach, I use the five steps to conscious creation superconscious transformation recode method to rewire the brain and recode your DNA. It is based on proven neuroscience, epigenetics, and quantum physics along side spiritual concepts of universal law and alchemy to help you release limiting beliefs, toxic emotions and resistance. This allows you to become an attraction magnet and move towards your desired reality in complete ease, grace, and flow

I'm also the Fearless Humble leader of Miracle Mavens helping moms create time & financial freedom. My personal mission is to transform the world one person at a time starting with myself

We are being dumbed down drugged up & disempowered & I am committed to helping people awaken to their full potential & raising the vibration of the planet to shift us into the new 5D paradigm "heaven on earth"

☼ Disclaimer ☼

I always encourage everyone to do their own research and form their own beliefs. Your beliefs are POWERFUL they create your reality. Take what resonates and leave the rest. If your beliefs are serving you well, if you are creating and living a life that you love or moving towards it, more power to you If not you've got to take a look at your mindset.

www.ingramcontent.com/pod-product-compliance
Lightning Source LLC
Chambersburg PA
CBHW070942120626
46546CB00004B/1532

* 9 7 8 1 9 6 8 0 6 1 1 2 8 *